songs of the peacock

words by Patrizia de Rachewiltz
pictures by Tien

 Paulist Press New York, N.Y. • Ramsey, N.J.

Library of Congress Catalogue Card Number: 77-83552
ISBN: 0-8091-2042-9 Paper
ISBN: 0-8091-0218-8 cloth

Published by: Paulist Press

Editorial Office: 1865 Broadway
New York, New York 10023

Business Office: 545 Island Road
Ramsey, New Jersey 07446

Printed and bound in the United States of America

CONTENTS

THE LONELY GOAT

In the middle of a very big field stood a tree.
It had blue flowers on its branches and beautiful
birds whose color turned from gold to golden
green.

And there, in the soft high grass, lived a white lonely
goat. Its only occupation was to choose the most
tender blades and listen to the enchanting songs of
the goldfinches. They sang soothingly of dancing
moons and joyful waves. This was the only world in
which the goat had ever lived, nothing else did it
know.

Completely happy, it breathed the morning air just
before the sun would rise, with no other thought
than to be pleased.

But one day something happened.

While the goat was nibbling at some tiny leaves, a
little girl came from the field.
As she had never seen a goat before, she stood there
and watched it with curious smiling eyes.
"Could it ever become her friend?" she thought.
So she picked a blue flower from the tree, the most
beautiful she could find, and gave it gracefully to the
goat.
But the goat did not see what she meant, and
surprised, stared at the flower. Then, greedily,
gulped it down.
As soon as the flower had disappeared, away
walked the little girl across the field, the weight of
her long golden braids being the only burden in
    her small life.

From that day on, the goat knew it was lonely. And it waited forever hoping that someone would hand it a beautiful blue flower from the tree.

9

TWO TINY TADPOLES

Two tiny little tadpoles came to life one sunny
April day, in a ditch by the waterfall.
They stared at each other, fascinated, and slipped
out of the soft water lily's net.
The first important thing they did was to give
themselves a name.
"You are Joy," said the more imaginative, squeezing
his little eyes for the great occasion. So Joy, happy to
have a name, waggled his tail and called his
companion Life.

11

Joy and Life touched the surface of the green sunny ditch. And in seeing the sky so far away and also so near when reflected in the water, they began to ponder over the mystery of the world.
"It gives us the unreachable!" they whispered in great surprise. And the sky above the water became their dream and the heaven under water became their home.

Their favorite game was to try to catch the passing
clouds, but they soon had to learn how to cope with
their ever changing moods. Because one day they
would be large and lovely, one day black and
menacing. But they were always unreachable, even
if they were so near to them.
It took a long time to understand their way of being
friends. Never did Joy and Life give up their game,
and they tried all the tricks that would come into
their heads.

So the more they thought, the more did their heads blow up, until they were as big as the moon reflected in the pond.
They did not try to catch the clouds anymore, or hope to live in their dreamy sky, but contented themselves to sing at night when it was all dark around the ditch.

And they whispered softly their beautiful names, in a sigh.

15

THE DWARF'S SIGH

The little dwarf of the wood, whose name was Risk, was caught one day in a cobweb among the branches of an oak tree.

This cobweb had been woven by the elf of loneliness, who passed from branch to branch, holding a very thin thread in his hand, so that he might not get lost.

In this cobweb Risk now was trapped and he knew he never could escape and stroll again in the big lovely woods. So Risk lay in the silvery net, surrounded by the silence of the trees. And to make himself comfortable he laced a hammock with the thin thread and tried to think of how to spend his lonely time.

17

The wind was blowing softly and the leaves were stirring. Risk realized that every thought of the big wood passed very close to the cobweb wherein he lay, and that he just had to stretch out his arm to catch them in his palm.

So he waited and waited, attentive to every sound of the wind. And suddenly he saw a little thought pass just above his head.

He leaned over as far as he could without losing his balance and finally held it tight in his hands. It was a beautiful thought, on its way to a far dark forest, and it was made of millions and millions of sparkling lights.

Risk held it so it would not escape, and turned it into
a dewdrop, delicate and transparent against the
light. Because of his great desire to be free again and
stroll in the wood, he wondered if the dewdrop
could help him.

He let it fall gently on the leaves below, in the hope
that the dewdrop might join the river and bring his
message to someone in the world.

And so it happened.

Just as the dewdrop touched the leaf, a gust of wind carried it off to the river where it followed the current. And a poet standing by the water, watching the sunset, beheld the tiny drop and understood its lamentations. He hurried to free Risk, who now can stroll again in his beloved wood, and the elf of loneliness will keep on passing from branch to branch, wondering why nobody ever falls in his net.

LEMONPIPS

It was the time when the hay lays abundant in the lazy fields, the time of long expected harvest. They came from the sun, three lemonpips, to visit Old Lady Mountain. And they found her seated in the trunk of an old tree, weaving time.
She saw them coming up the steep path, so she made a knot in her invisible thread and sat motionless waiting for them to reach the dead tree trunk.

23

The three lemonpips bowed graciously and sat at her feet. I, You and He were their names and they had come a long way from the sun to see the Old Lady. I said, "Gracious Lady of the Mountain, will you tell me the secret of joy?"
Lady Mountain fixed her eyes on the distant horizon and they twinkled with sunshine. She smiled and said, "Once you have found it, treasure it most preciously, and above all prize the way to find it."
I thanked her and went to sit on a rock to think over her words.

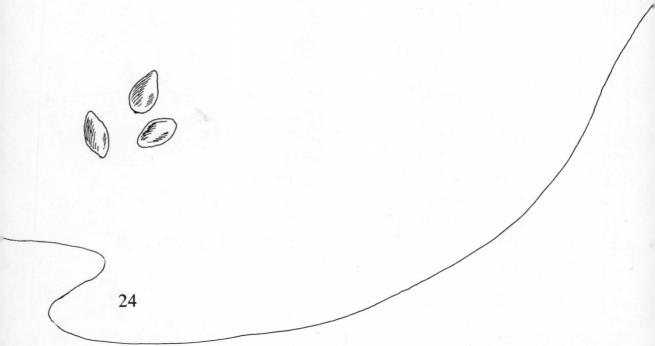

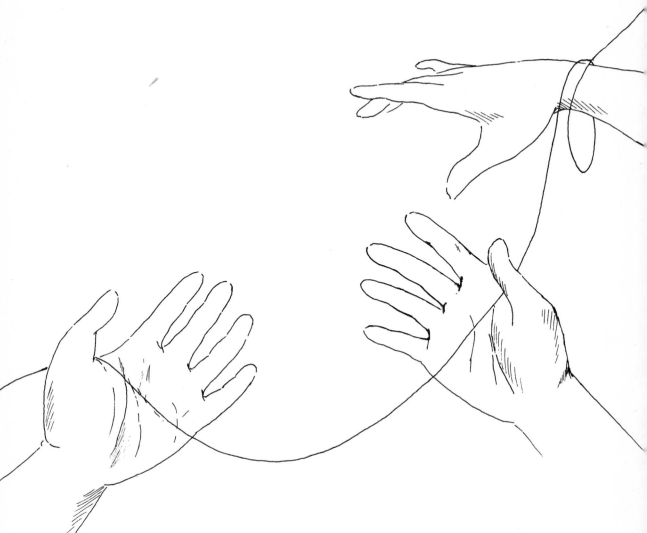

You asked, "Gracious Lady of the Mountain, will
you tell me the secret of humility?"
Lady Mountain glanced at her hands which still held
the thread of time and You saw deep lines in them,
deep lines which showed patient work and
forgotten vanity.
You saw in them the answer, thanked her, and went
to sit on a rock by his friend.

At last He asked, "Gracious Lady of the Mountain, will you tell me the secret of patience?"
Lady Mountain closed her eyes and sighed. She took the thread and began slowly to weave again, as she had always done.

He joined the others and together the three
lemonpips danced around the Old Lady of the
Mountain, before vanishing back into the sun.

27

THE DEER
WITH A THOUSAND HORNS

F ar away, in the mountains of snow and
moonlight, lived the deer with a
thousand horns.
He was beautiful and proud and wandered along the
lonely paths, leaving his footprints that winds
scattered over swaying trees.
He was the deer of the rising moon.

29

One wintery night, in his sleep, he had a dream. He dreamt he was standing on the highest mountain peak, when a voice whispered into his ear, "Can you jump high enough to reach the moon?"
Surprised, he stared at the perfect blade of light, so bright and yet so pale, suspended in blue air.
He took a deep breath and jumped. Swift he traveled through immense starlit spaces, so high his horns touched the moon.

He awoke shivering. Had he wallowed in the snow or had he patted the new moon? Of one thing he was certain: his horns had blossomed into a thousand silvery moon-cusps.

From that day he lived his dream. He had jumped higher than any deer ever had. Now he ran on his dearest paths and heard the trees whisper, "Look at his beautiful horns!" and the rivers answered, "How brightly they shine!"

And he passed by, happy and proud, and never told them of his secret journey to the moon. He alone was the deer with a thousand horns.

Then spring came. The woods changed into greenest moss and the frost melted.

One day, as he was playfully trying to catch the rays
of sunlight between the trees, a delicate tune
reached his ears, the air seemed filled by it. He lifted
his regal head and listened. Never before had he
heard this music and he wondered which mountain,
for there were only mountains all around him, had
such a beautiful voice.

He stood still and the music floated tinkling like
water drops. He knew all the mountains, all their
rivers and woods, he knew them all, but this
mountain which sang so lovingly he did not know.
He searched all over, he climbed the highest peaks,
up up to the very top of dangerous rocks, but he
never seemed to come nearer to the music which
danced through the air.

"Where could this mountain be?" the deer
wondered, after days and days of leaping and
running, crossing distances he had never seen,
climbing heights above the clouds, cold windy
peaks.
At night he could no longer sleep, so compelling was
the music in his heart.

35

And then, one day, when he had almost lost all hope of finding the musical mountain, a bird with golden wings spoke to him and said, "You looked everywhere, in all the woods and on every peak. Did you not know that I always sat on your beautiful horns, singing the song of the rising moon?"

As soon as the bird had spoken, the deer was filled
with joy. Now he knew he would not have to seek on
dangerous mountain peaks the happiness he had
within.

TSUKI SAN (MISTER MOON)

A little light was shining over the bent shoulders of an old Chinese scribe.
Lady Night entered his small garden and slipped in through the open window.
Plum petals were in the air.
He dipped the delicate brush in the black ink and his hand rested awhile in magic suspense, as he wondered, "What sign shall I give to the sun?"

39

As it was already so late, his hand drew a very
simple form in four strokes. A pale smile appeared
on his wrinkled face as the little sun sign
flew out of the window to shine at the other end
of the world.
Then it was time to draw a sign for the moon. But the
old scribe was so tired. Lady Night had already
closed her eyes and the sandman had sprinkled
sleep in every flower of the garden.

His shoulders were almost touching the white sheet
of rice-paper, still empty, but his mind still wanted
to work. He knew sun and moon were brothers and
shone together to bring light and warmth to the
earth.

So he thought it proper to draw them with the same sign. He dipped his brush in the black ink. But his hand was so tired that the two first strokes dropped on the sheet of paper with less control, and he noticed with disappointment that they were much longer than he had intended.

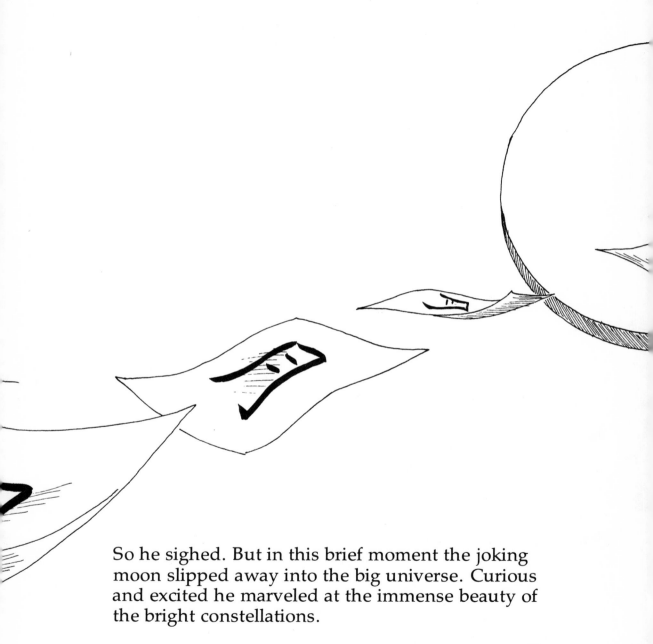

So he sighed. But in this brief moment the joking moon slipped away into the big universe. Curious and excited he marveled at the immense beauty of the bright constellations.

Only at dawn did he return, exhausted by his adventure, into the hands of the scribe, who had waited in anger all night long. He watched the little moon with severe eyes and said, "I shall not draw you like the sun, you shall never be as your brother who gives warmth day and night. You will only shine when it's dark, and you'll be cold like gold can be."

Since that night the little moon is pale with sadness
and falls in love with every melancholic heart on
earth which dreams at night.

45

THE SILVER FLUTE

Two grasshoppers were sitting in the grass, on a warm summer evening.
The day was fading into the scented border of the field. Shadows swayed among the silhouettes of this green infinity. Nothing stirred in the air.
But somewhere, invisible almost, perceived through fern fringes, the two grasshoppers were chit-chatting gaily cheek to cheek. Both young, they moved their long slender feelers according to the mood of their talk.

And thus it could be seen that one of them held in his
tiny hands the most beautiful flute that ever had
existed. A flute as light and thin as a satin thread,
almost transparent with subtle designs carved in
silvery lines. And the tunes it produced swelled his
friend's heart, oh how he wanted this flute.
He yearned to possess it and play for all the bees and
flowers and all the spiders in the field.

He would have given his life for it.

The day had passed in excited bargaining, yet no
decision had been taken by the two little friends and
the flute was still in its owner's hands.
"It's time we come to an agreement," one of the
grasshoppers finally said to his friend. "I know you
wish to have this precious flute of mine with all your
heart, so it's your heart you'll have to give me in
exchange. No other price could reward a gift like
this."

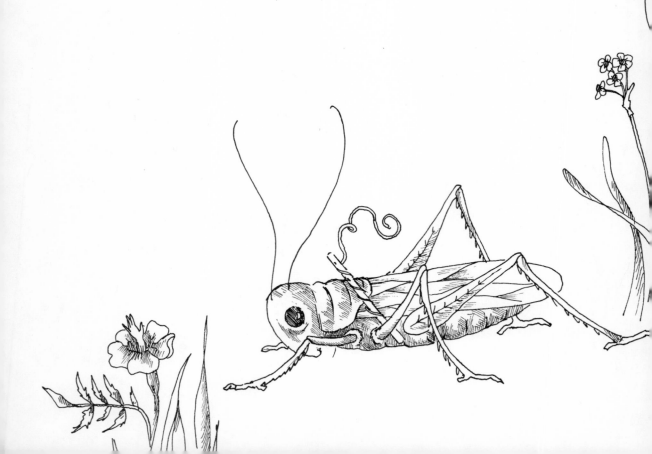

With a happy smile his companion said in content whisper, "You can have my heart, if this is your wish!" So the two grasshoppers under the fern fringes embraced and departed, each with his new wonderful gift.

Years and seasons went by.
Yet the bees were as busy as ever on white and yellow flowercups, the spiders weaved their threads from stem to stem. Nothing had changed in the big field, and nobody paid the least attention to a lonely grasshopper with a silver flute, because no music came from it. The only tune he was able to play was monotonous and sad.
So on and on the grasshopper went, jumping and playing the single tune that never ceased to tell him that for it he had lost his heart.

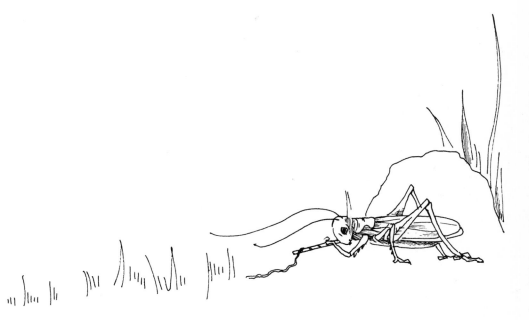

Maybe, he is still looking for it on warm summer
evenings, among the green grass of the field.

THE FORGOTTEN SEED

On a grey rock, where the winds blew with all their might, stood a castle. Its towers against the sky challenged the swift clouds that hung low and menacing. And after tempest, the walls glittered with raindrops and the light around it was a halo of peace.

In this castle lived, all by herself, a beautiful lady. Her love and care went to her garden, where red and blue flowers mingled with all kinds of scented herbs. Evergreens grew by the walls, holding on for life with such force that no tempest could have torn them from their strong hold.

In the evening all the birds came to the tower and
sang their lively songs for the beautiful lady.
She sat motionless and listened, her eyes turned
toward the valley, and the birds came closer and
flew over her head in swirling dances.

In a wooden box she kept a seed. Someone had given it to her a long time ago, never revealing its nature. So it had remained closed in the cherished box for years and years.

It was one of those evenings when she sat listening intently to the birds, and the air seemed filled with such expectations, that she suddenly decided to fetch the long forgotten seed.
She did so, and thereafter devoted her time completely to the care of the new little green plant that had sprouted and that grew so rapidly.

The tiny leaves became larger and larger, the plant grew higher and higher, and the beautiful lady was proud and excited in seeing her seed turn out to be such a friend. Yet she still didn't guess its nature. It grew tall and it grew large and she was so pleased with its company. She sat near it now most of the time, fancying every morning to see its fruits whose taste would be as honey.

But no fruit ever appeared. Instead, the leaves were spreading out over the whole tower, creeping on the grey walls, taking inch by inch every bit of space. Until it closed all around her, a prison of thick green foliage from which she could never have escaped.

From that day the birds sang of a beautiful lady,
captured by a long forgotten seed.

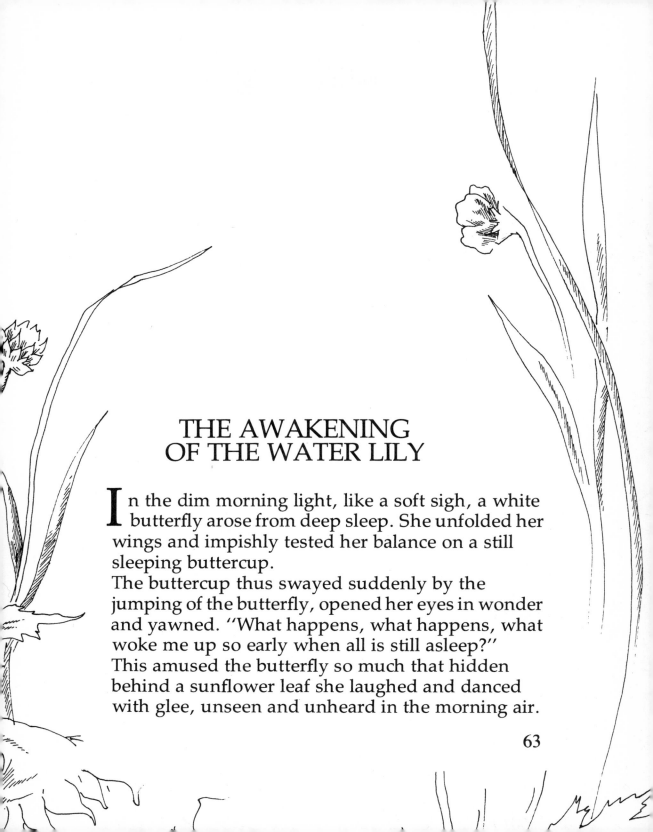

THE AWAKENING
OF THE WATER LILY

In the dim morning light, like a soft sigh, a white butterfly arose from deep sleep. She unfolded her wings and impishly tested her balance on a still sleeping buttercup.

The buttercup thus swayed suddenly by the jumping of the butterfly, opened her eyes in wonder and yawned. "What happens, what happens, what woke me up so early when all is still asleep?" This amused the butterfly so much that hidden behind a sunflower leaf she laughed and danced with glee, unseen and unheard in the morning air.

One by one each buttercup awoke in the same astonished wonder, while the little butterfly giggled in her swift hidings, amused and excited by her morning game.

Then she discovered the water pond. The grass was a velvet carpet all around it, the stillness was such as to leave the butterfly breathless for a moment. The water was transparent as a mirror, and at the bottom of it she could see the tiny fishes sleeping and weeds curled up in gentle repose.

65

She stood motionless and breathed in all the peace of this scenery. But how could all still be asleep, she thought, when life was so short, so quick, that you couldn't miss even an instant of it?

Then, just ready to break into laughter and wake everyone up, her eyes caught sight of a sleeping beauty floating on the water. All in white, it was the most wonderful image she had ever seen. "It must be a butterfly just like me," she thought, "that fell asleep on the pond. I must wake her up fast, she'll come with me all over the fields and play with the buttercups . . . . "

Through the soft touch of wings, the water lily awoke. "Come with me!" the butterfly laughed, amused by the other's laziness and astonishment. And blinded by her own joy of living, flitting from flower to flower, she fancied that her new friend would catch up with her; she fluttered off heedless toward other sleeping buttercups. She didn't give herself time to think and did not hear the sigh of the water lily, who was attached to the muddy bottom of the pond.

That morning on waking up, the lily was sad
because it could not fly.

THE WINGED KITE

The field was wide and golden under the first
sunrays of the morning. The little boy ran
joyfully across the grass and through the bushes of
wild roses, and he held tightly a beautiful kite,
painted with all the colors of the rainbow. The name
of the little boy was Wing and he had given the same
name to his precious kite.
As soon as he reached an open space, he stopped
and searched the sky for the direction of the wind.
Then he unwound slowly, almost ceremoniously,
the long thread that he held in his hands. Suddenly,
up up soared the kite toward the soft-clouded sky,
swaying gently in the brisk air of the morning.

Wing's eyes followed it with excitement, while he kept running on the grass, watching his steps through the bushes and at the same time looking up to his beloved kite.

In a moment the kite was a tiny vivid spot in the distant sky and Wing kept singing, "Tell me, tell me what do you see up there? Are there palaces on the clouds and silver stars that always glow? Tell me, what do you see up there?"

73

His voice ran excited in the space he had created between the kite and himself, and the little end of the thread was the only link with his friend. He knew that if it slipped away he would never know about the wonders that existed so far away. But he was staring so lovingly at every movement of the kite, that he forgot to look where he was putting his feet.

He suddenly stumbled headlong over a bush of wild roses.

75

When he got up as fast as he could, he felt a pain in his hand and he saw that it was bleeding. A thorn had pierced his finger and when he looked up he could just see the little end of the thread going higher and higher out of his reach.

His kite was gone, gone to the vast skies and stars and would not come back to tell him of the wonders it had seen.

So Wing sat down and cried softly and evening
came.
He fell asleep and was awakened by a gentle rain
dripping on his sleepy eyes.

77

He jumped up and ran across the field. Then, the sun fought its way through the grey clouds and on the horizon appeared, to his surprise, a beautiful rainbow.

"My kite, my kite," he cried out laughing. "It has not deserted me." "How lovely it is. How they shine, all the blues and greens I painted on it."

And happy, he ran toward the spot where he
imagined one end of the rainbow touched the field.
But all he could do was to admire those shining
colors, and he rejoiced because he knew he had
made such a beautiful rainbow out of his beloved
kite.

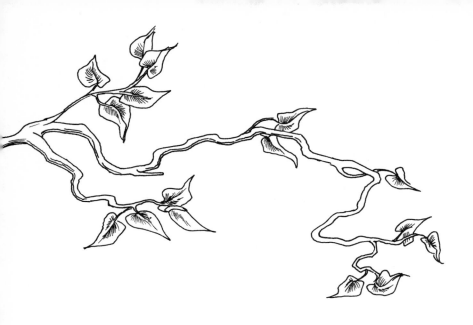

THE SILENT PARROT

In a beautiful garden by the sea, where soft winds whispered from tree to tree, lived the silent parrot. He was kept in a cage superbly adorned, placed on top of an evergreen hill, overlooking the bay, in the shadow of golden leaves.

Far away the horizon vanished behind an enormous rock which seemed almost to pierce the sky.

But even among so much beauty, the parrot had never given a sign of joy, had never whispered a single little word, and this brought sadness to the proud Lady She, who owned the parrot, the bay and the golden tree.

Lady She's greatest sorrow was the silence of her parrot, and she sat by the cage under the glittering leaves and sang with modulated voice, hoping the parrot would imitate her.

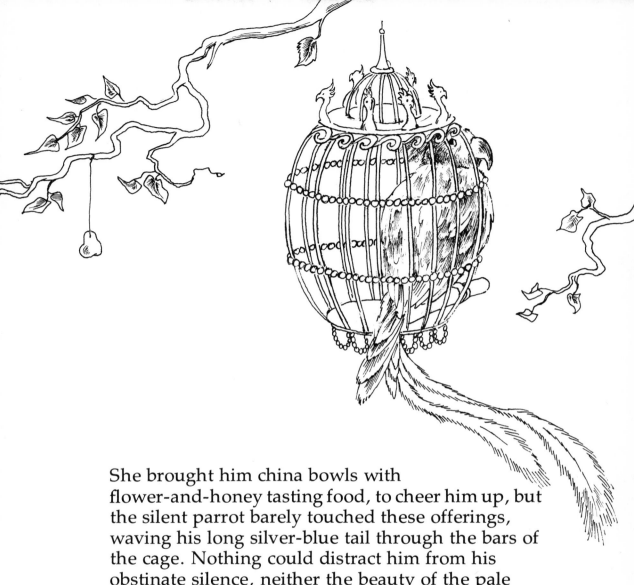

She brought him china bowls with
flower-and-honey tasting food, to cheer him up, but
the silent parrot barely touched these offerings,
waving his long silver-blue tail through the bars of
the cage. Nothing could distract him from his
obstinate silence, neither the beauty of the pale
waters and the golden tree, nor the exotic gifts Lady
She gave him, nor the songs of sunset. The rays
of the moon softly played on the silk dress
embroidered with magnificent golds and greens and
on the jewels that hung around the neck and on the
fingers of the beautiful Lady.

So the years passed away, in the garden by the silent bay, and She kept longing for a beloved word. Feeling lonely and sad, She cried softly while the wind blew among the leaves.

Then one day, in her sleep, She dreamed she had
opened the iron door of the parrot's cage, and he had
flown on the branches of the golden tree, praising
with all the words that She had taught him the
beauty of the morning.

85

When Lady She awoke she ran up the hill and reached the cage out of breath, but to her great surprise the little door was wide open and the parrot was nowhere to be seen.

She called him by all the most beloved names, she searched everywhere in the green garden, but could not find him.

Desperately Lady She cried and the wind came to
dry her tears, and suddenly she heard a piercing cry
of joy from a nearby tree. It was the parrot singing all
the words he had learned from her.

He praised the beauties of the sea and of the moon, and Lady She threw the golden cage into the water and listened and talked to her beloved parrot whom she could neither touch nor see anymore.

Every little word of his made her happy and proud,
in her beautiful garden by the sea, with the parrot
and her golden tree.

THE STAR CARVER

In a small mountain village, one could hear at all times of the day and night, the gay hammering of the woodcarver and a voice singing softly of the beautiful stars.

If somebody stopped to watch the man working, he could see him in deep concentration, bent over his piece of wood and he wouldn't stop singing, nor would he lift his head to greet the wanderer, but would go on carving with agile fingers.

He wasn't unkind, but when he worked, his mind always slipped into another world and he forgot all reality.

91

His work was to carve round shaped wooden blocks, and each of them he shaped in his one and favorite form, that of a star. That's why in the small mountain village they called him "the happy star carver."

Those who passed by his little hut and saw him concentrated on his work, smiled and shook their heads thinking, "That man wants to bring the stars on this poor earth. But it's not gold he is carving. Let him dream, his illusions are not very profitable, but he seems content."

His village friends thought the same, but he never listened to them or joined them in their nightly carousing. But when everything was asleep and only the starlight shone on his table, he kept on working and, looking up, sighed deeply, "Could I, oh could I bring you all down on this earth to make us happy . . . ." He was certain that as soon as he had finished carving a star, far away in the lit-up sky a real star would leave the others and cross the firmament in a shiny glow, and fall somehwere on the earth.

The songs of the star carver wandered at night in the small village with the lightness of a dream.

One day he decided to count all the wooden stars he had carved and he was convinced that the stars he was counting were those missing in the sky. "Hundred and seven, hundred and eight, hundred and nine . . . ." His hut glittered with stars while his voice counted excitedly, but that very moment a rich merchant entered, greeting loudly, "Hey young man, I want to buy, I want to buy all your work, I think they'll fit well the mansion I just bought near the big city."

The star carver stopped counting and watched the merchant with wide-open eyes. And his gaze ran from him to the thousand silver coins on the table. And so it happened that he was left without a single wooden star and a lot of money in his pocket.

97

The day the villagers saw the sign "Closed" hanging on the door of the hut, they imagined that the star carver had at last given up his unprofitable work and was now looking for something else.

98

Years later they heard from gossip that a poor young
man had suddenly become rich, that he had made a
big fortune nobody knew how, and that he traveled
from one exotic city of the world to the other, and
they whispered with excitement, "What a lucky,
lucky man!"

THE PEACOCK'S SONG

I f one looked in the Lady's garden, one saw her
seated very gracefully on the back of her beautiful
peacock. She was named Lady of the mirror,
because she spent her time with her friend, holding
in her hand a tiny mirror, wherein she contemplated
herself for long hours.
She had no other concern in life, no greater joy than
being admired. Her long embroidered dress fell in
large folds of colors over the white feathers of the
peacock, one of her hands touching gently the
elegant neck of the king of birds.

In the little garden full of scents and flowers, she asked in singing tones what the peacock saw in the mirror, and always came the answer, "What a beauty, what a beauty!"

This made the Lady blush with pleasure and she held up her face to the summer breeze, feeling a thrill of pride at the compliments of her dear friend. At times, a sunray fell on the mirror and made an extraordinary light diffuse all around them like a halo of gold.

103

The summer passed slowly in the garden of the Lady
of the mirror and always did the peacock answer
her, "What a beauty I see!"

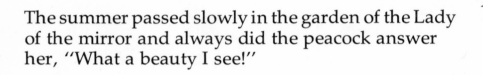

The flowers turned pale and the leaves began to glitter in orange-red colors. The peacock saw the slow approach of autumn by the way birds began to gather in the sky, before leaving for distant countries. And he followed their flight with a sigh, unheard by the Lady, for he was her friend and he had to stay with her, for once she had saved his life.

But each time he saw his image, for it was his image he saw and not his Lady's, his heart swelled with joy at his beautiful head, his proud neck, his bright feathers. And when the Lady asked him what he saw, he couldn't repress his pride and always charmed himself by saying those tender words. Never did the Lady guess that he didn't see her but his own image in the mirror she held up so lovingly.

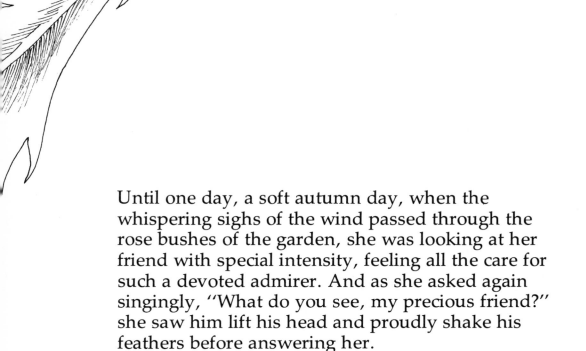

Until one day, a soft autumn day, when the whispering sighs of the wind passed through the rose bushes of the garden, she was looking at her friend with special intensity, feeling all the care for such a devoted admirer. And as she asked again singingly, "What do you see, my precious friend?" she saw him lift his head and proudly shake his feathers before answering her.

Thus to her great surprise she discovered with a pain that tore her heart, that what he saw was not her beauty but his own, his own selfish beautiful eyes. She felt anger and sadness and her feelings were so hurt she threw the mirror violently against the garden wall where it splintered into a thousand little glass pieces, never to be one again, and never to reflect her face again on warm summer evenings. She felt sad for the behavior of her friend, and he could not help wondering why the Lady had broken the mirror wherein he had liked to stare so joyfully.

Almost unconsciously, they began to look at each
other with other eyes, astonished, and the peacock
saw how really beautiful his Lady was and the Lady
had the same thoughts about her friend. They faced
each other and discovered that they were both
beautiful in each other's eyes.

109

Their friendship deepened and they strolled in the fresh wintery garden with more affection than ever. They didn't need a mirror anymore to tell them the truth, their eyes met.

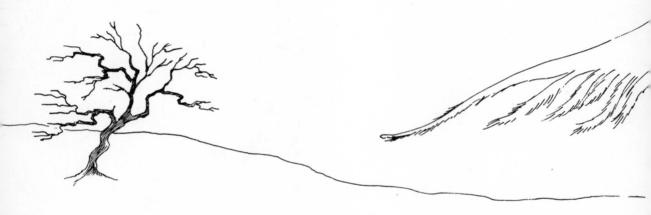

And the arms of the Lady closed tightly around her friend's long neck, feeling it warm and friendly, and the peacock felt like the king of this realm, lucky to carry on his back such a lovely, lovely Lady.

112

THE TEASING CROWS

Two pitch black crows sat on a wire by the road. Below them a big field stretched out full of the richest golden corn. The sun had not yet risen and the two crows were still half asleep, perched on the wire in the silence of the morning.

Then the old farmer came slowly across the field, as every morning, to work his land. And looking up he saw them, waiting, two black spots against the sky. "Oh, just wait," he whispered. "One of these days I'll get you, staring there at my field and making fun of me! I know very well that as soon as I am gone you will dare ravage my corn, but just wait, I'll get you . . . . ."

He hung his hat on a bush nearby and the first
sunrays stretched over the big field. "Caw, caw,
caw," the two crows began to laugh and laugh,
jumping clumsily on the wire by the road. The
farmer got all red in the face, thinking as usual that
they were laughing at his words.
Then the sun showed itself fully and the day of work
slowly went by, the farmer bent over his land and
the two black crows always perched above him,
suspiciously looking down.

As evening came and the field was filled with
shadows, the farmer picked up his hat and, glancing
once more at the two crows, went away saying, "So
long, I'll get you, just wait!"
And every morning it was the same "Caw, caw,
caw," and the farmer worked all through the
summer season, with the two black crows sitting
there and staring at him, waiting.

115

Sometimes he would look up suddenly just as the sun was rising, and shout at them, but "Caw, caw, caw," the crows just laughed at him and this made him furious and he would not look up again for the rest of the day.

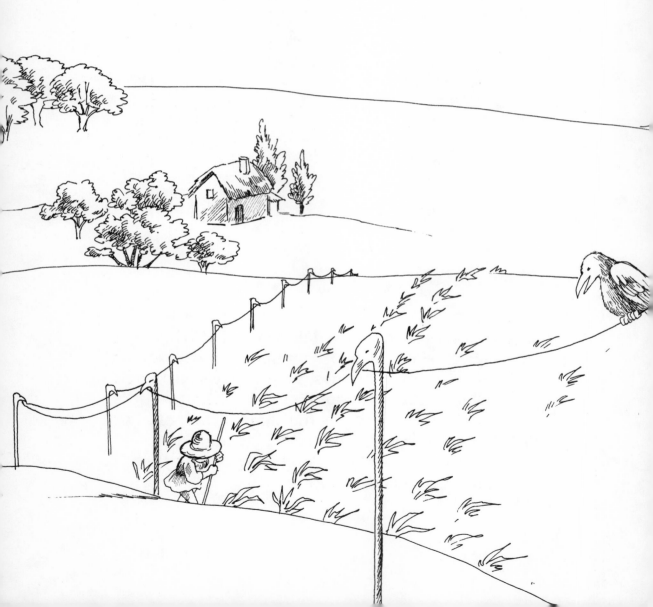

But in a way, it was the only company he had during his hard labor, and he certainly would have missed them if one morning they were gone. They were part of the landscape and there was no one else to shout at. But at their "Caw, caw, caw," he always got enraged and he wondered why they laughed so much, having fun at his expense.

117

So one day he decided to spy on them and see whether they would laugh as much if he weren't there. That morning he took another path and hid in a bush near the field.

Suddenly he heard the same old high pitched "Caw, caw, caw," and saw them balanced on the wire as usual, laughing and laughing. "They must have seen me," he thought full of anger, "they saw me and now they'll always laugh at my failure to fool them."

So he went home that day and threw himself on his bed, furious, and thought of what he could do. He was by nature rough and hard working and one seldom saw a smile on his wrinkled face.
He jumped out of bed, decided to try out his plan.
He went to the field and acted as though nothing had happened.

119

When the crows began to laugh, and this time it seemed that their "Caw, caw, caw," would never stop, he looked up and haunched in the same position as the two black crows, he roared with laughter until tears came to his eyes and he almost choked.
But he laughed more and more in seeing the baffled faces of his two friends.

That morning the two crows decided to fly to a
bigger corn field, and while leaving the farmer still
laughing, they proudly said to each other, "Anyway
he wouldn't have understood that we never laughed
at him, but at the sun tickling us under our
wings . . . . "

LILLIPUT LEE

Lilliput Lee was an ageless tiny man. He was so small that he had to stand on a rock to unlatch the gate of his garden.

He had built his own house, where everything was within reach, a dwarf's table and chair, on which he hopped with a swift movement and a tiny bed with a soft pillow and wooden frame.

Lilliput Lee was very tidy, and he always got upset when his friend Lilliput Lipp came to see him. Lipp had the habit of sitting on Lee's bed, but as he was so fat he couldn't step out of it again without help, and so he just rolled from one side to the other, laughing and puffing. But he was of gentle nature and everybody was amused by his endless jokes.

123

Lilliput Lee's garden was full of treasures he had found in the mountains. Brilliant and shiny stones. He had been a rock-searcher for a long time and would be a rock-searcher for another long, long time. Because even if his hair was bushy and his eyes looked tired at times, one couldn't have guessed his age. Everybody in Lilliput Land lived on, celebrating hundreds of birthdays.

It was a very happy and busy land, and almost everyone was a rock-searcher. They left home early at dawn, when the white pale moon still lingered in the sky, and returned after darkness had fallen, with their rock-sacks filled with all those beautiful precious rocks.

The steps that led to the front door of Lilliput Lee's house were smooth and polished from constantly stepping on them.

125

One early morning Lilliput Lee left as usual at the crack of dawn, locked his door and started marching toward the big mountain. He loved to go alone on these trips, so he could lie down whenever it pleased him, on the soft moss of the woods. He knew better than anyone else where the most precious diamonds were hidden, he knew all the treasures in the deepest caves, but in all those years he had kept a secret.

At times it weighed upon him and he was tempted to run to his discovered queen of diamonds, to make sure he had not just dreamed about it. But there it was, magnificent, a sight that took away his breath and whose brilliant glimmer blinded his eyes. When he looked at it in amazement, a voice always whispered to him, "Don't touch me or else you'll fall, fall, fall . . . . "

Lilliput Lee had kept this secret for many years.
That morning his steps took him to the dangerous
hidden spot.

He felt excited and happy and a little bit scared. He
had awakened with a strange threatening feeling
and now he was waiting for the voice to whisper
those terrible words. The woods seemed perfectly
still, as if the invisible guardians of the queen of
diamonds were asleep. But Lilliput Lee knew it
wasn't so. He approached nearer than he had ever
done, his heart beating rapidly in his chest.

Now he stood in the forbidden circle of silvery light. Unconsciously he covered his ears so as not to hear the threatening voice.

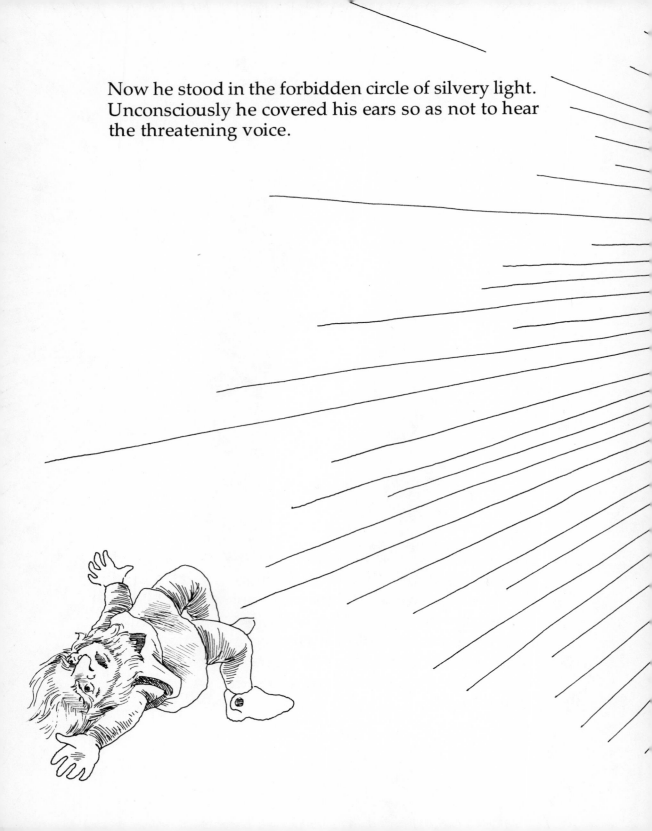

And then he lost his head. The trees began to swirl about him, and while he felt himself thrown through miles and miles of distances, in an endless fall, he knew he had looked into the most precious and dangerous diamond of the world. And he disappeared that morning, never to come back again. Nobody ever knew what Lilliput Lee had seen.

131

Weeds and bushes grew over his little house and soon nobody remembered that once a home had stood there, with polished little steps leading to the front door.

Only a bird always sat on a bush nearby, singing the story of Lilliput Lee. But for everyone it was just mere singing.

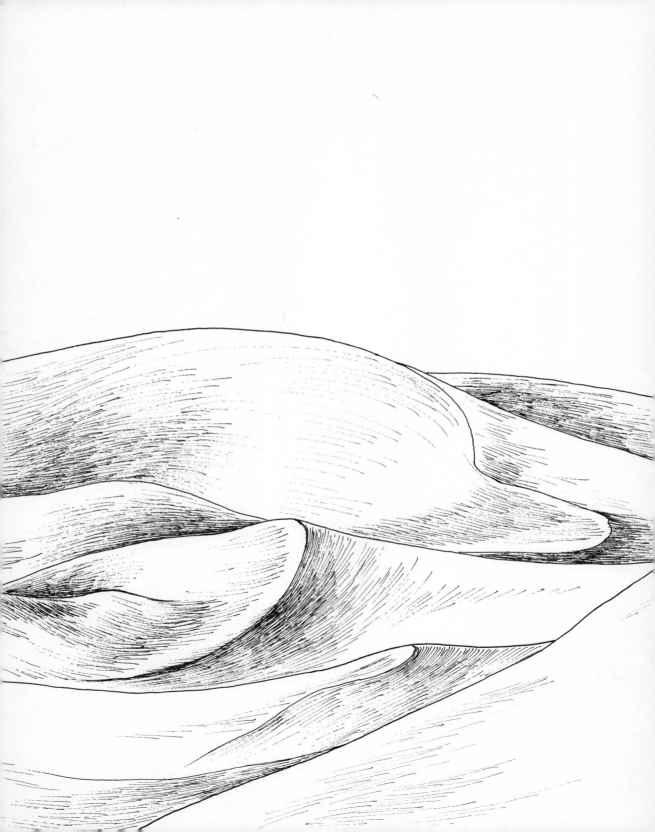

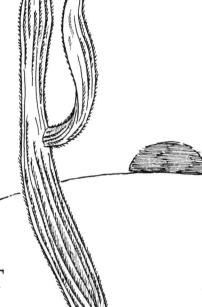

THE POET
OF THE DESERT

O ne day, a tiny green cactus was born among the
    sand dunes of the big, big desert.
It grew up all by himself, under the hot sun and the
thorns grew faster and faster over his proud head.
He was sure this was a sign of distinguished
intelligence. He recited verses he remembered from
childhood in a loud voice.
He dreamt of a big audience all around him,
clapping their hands at his words, but as soon as he
had finished his outburst of eloquence, there was
nobody to applaud him or to tell him to go on.

But he wasn't unhappy in the big desert all by
himself. Because he had a loyal friend who was his
audience and his critic and who never left him alone.

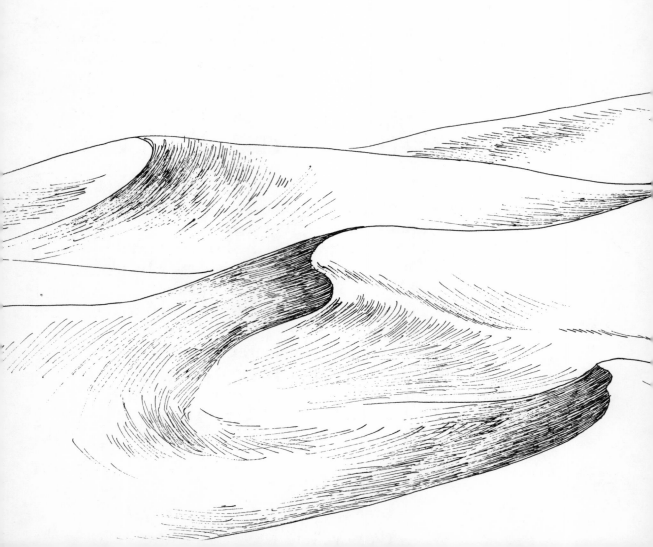

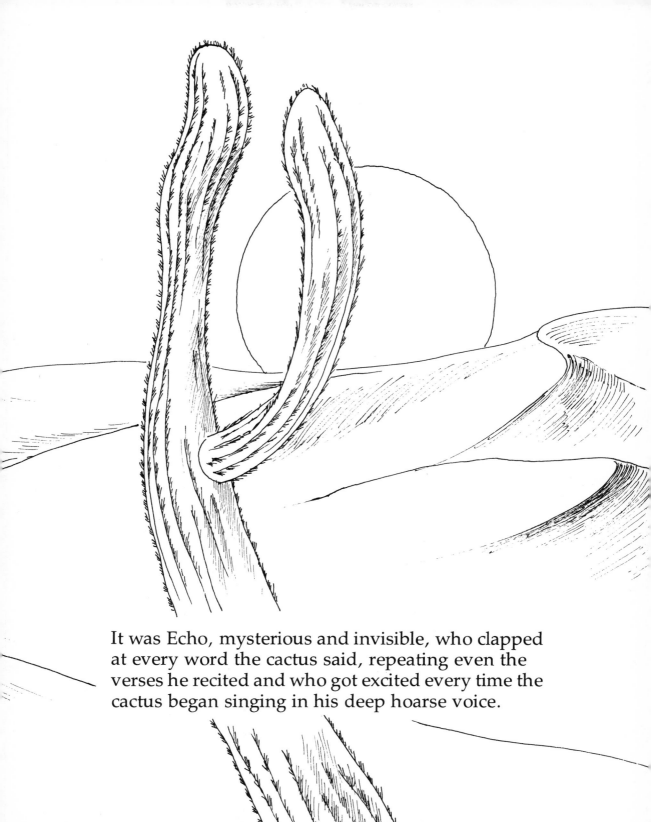

It was Echo, mysterious and invisible, who clapped
at every word the cactus said, repeating even the
verses he recited and who got excited every time the
cactus began singing in his deep hoarse voice.

The sun was very hot and shone all day long over the sand dunes.

When the wind came to visit the tiny green cactus, blowing with all its might, the sand danced in the air and made him laugh and laugh, holding his arms over his head. He felt strong with all his sharp thorns, and no wind could harm him. Besides, he loved the wind, the confusion, the dancing sand around him.

Nothing ever happened otherwise in the big desert and the visit of Mister Wind always excited his poetic mind.

At times, a bird flew down and rested beside him and chatted about all the countries and people he had seen. This pleased the cactus who listened attentively, trying to fit in a verse here and there or a quotation from one of his favorite poets.

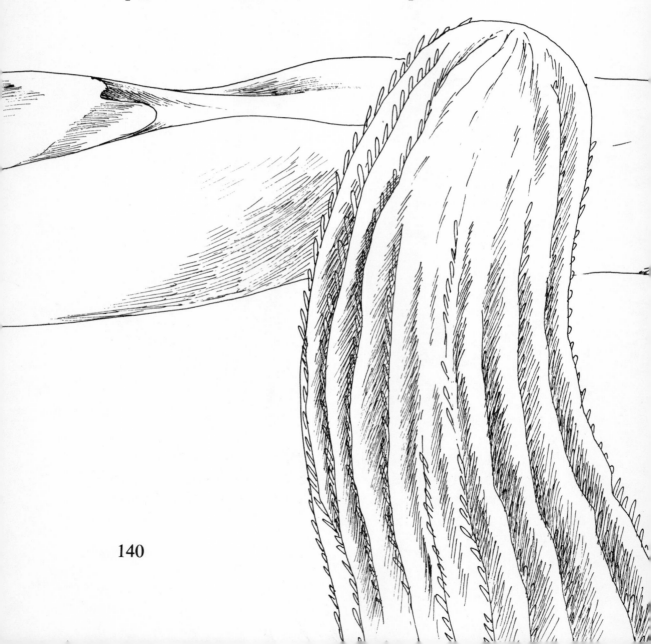

He was a born poet, he composed his own verses and speeches and he was certain that everybody in the world at the other end of the desert could hear him and praise his style and capacity.

He lived in the illusion he needed, to accept his
solitary life. There were times when he just stared at
the space around and was taken by the urge to
wander. But then he thought that by staying put on
his own roots he could achieve perfection.
Time was precious and he had to avoid the
temptations of the unknown.

One morning his mind was filled with poetic images, and he was wrinkling his forehead in concentration, keeping his eyes closed, when suddenly he sang in a loud and assured voice, "I am the poet of the desert . . . ." But at that point he was interrupted by his friend Echo, who dared, in these same words, to let him believe he was the poet of the desert.

The cactus grew paler and paler, he couldn't and wouldn't believe the challenge and the offense of his once so dear friend.
So he took in a big breath and shouted still louder: "I am the poet . . . . "

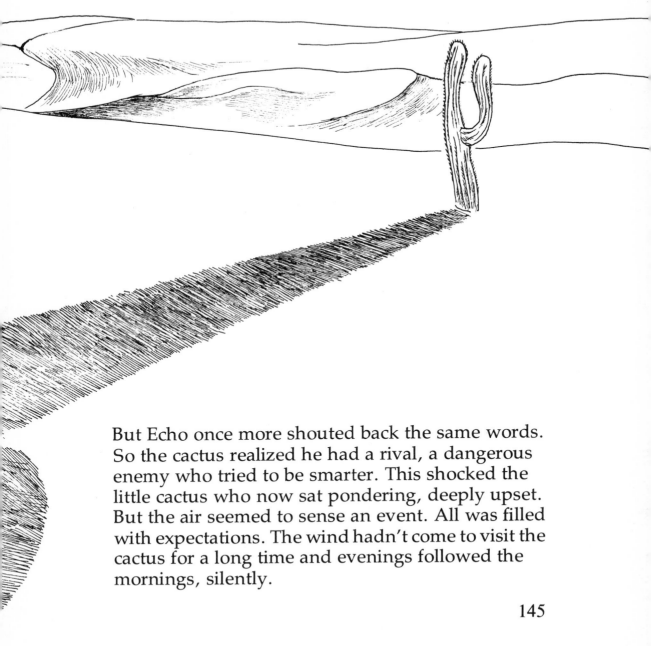

But Echo once more shouted back the same words.
So the cactus realized he had a rival, a dangerous
enemy who tried to be smarter. This shocked the
little cactus who now sat pondering, deeply upset.
But the air seemed to sense an event. All was filled
with expectations. The wind hadn't come to visit the
cactus for a long time and evenings followed the
mornings, silently.

Then, one day, as the sun was just setting, casting a pink velvet light over the sand, a storm of wind came up suddenly and the air seemed filled with sparkling lightenings.

In the morning all was still and calm. It was the most wonderful morning of the desert, the air as pure as crystal and the sand as soft as an illusion.

And there stood the tiny green cactus all by himself. But on his head the most splendid yellow flower had blossomed as from his own heart. It was the happiest day of his life. He stopped shouting his verses to the wind, but kept them in his heart, and so every new verse became one of those splendid golden flowers with which he now is covered.

THE MERMAID'S DREAM

The sea was calm and endless, that night of full moon. It seemed as if dreams danced in the moonlight above the water, in the form of three beautiful ladies, dressed in white foam and with silvery stars in their hair. They danced and sang with voices that reached all those who were still awake. They sang words that could only be understood by the mermaids who lived at the bottom of the sea.

149

One of these was a very young mermaid, with long dark hair that covered her shoulders down to the waist. Her greatest joy was to float gently on the waves on nights of the full moon. And there watch the stars and listen to the three white ladies. She had one only dream: to dance as those ladies above the sea and sing with their beautiful voices. Those nights passed slowly and the moon would disappear in the calm light of dawn.

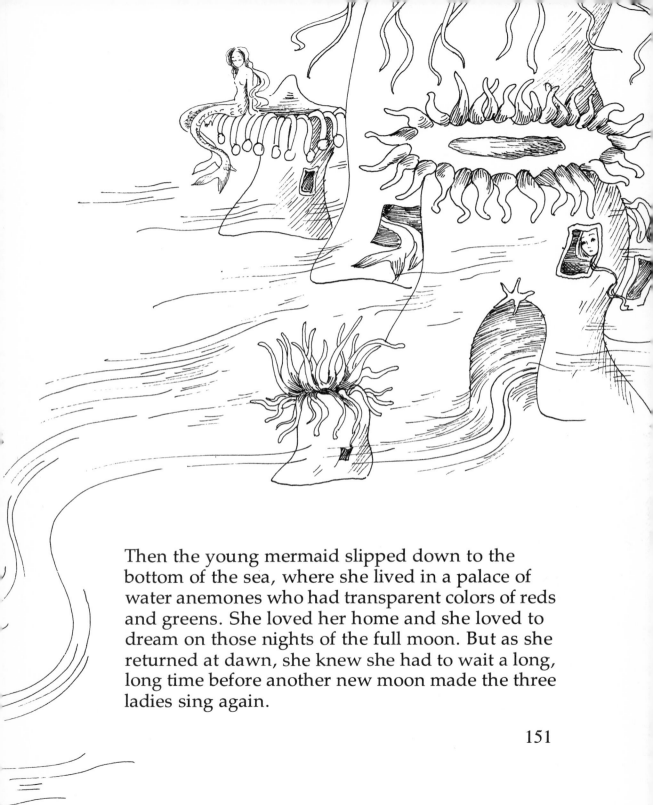

Then the young mermaid slipped down to the
bottom of the sea, where she lived in a palace of
water anemones who had transparent colors of reds
and greens. She loved her home and she loved to
dream on those nights of the full moon. But as she
returned at dawn, she knew she had to wait a long,
long time before another new moon made the three
ladies sing again.

She had a father whom she adored and whose tales filled her with excitement. Her mother was the Lady of the Green, a beautiful mermaid whose hair was so long it curled around every green rock and plant, down, down at the bottom of the sea. She also had six sisters, who played games with each other and didn't care to float above the waters and listen to the three white ladies.

Her only brother was very dear to her, but he had left one day to go and fight the monsters of Dream Island. He had never returned and many years had passed since the day he had left.

And the little mermaid longed for the day he would come home again, riding proudly on the back of a silvery dolphin.

Three seasons had passed and all was calm and uneventful. But one night, a night of full moon, the little mermaid was watching the dream-ladies, dancing gracefully and singing with voices that broke her heart with longings.

So she fell into a sort of languid trance. She dozed off above the waters, and when dawn came she didn't hurry as usual to the bottom of the sea, for she was sound asleep. A soft sleep had held her back and she drifted off, taken by the currents, and was thrown on to the shores of Dream Island.

Here she awoke and she saw the sun for the first time. All was so bright, the light burned her eyes and tears streamed down her cheeks, burning her face. Many a time had she heard of the beauty of Dream Island, of its dangers and its power.
She lay on the shore and felt pain in her body. She knew the sun was burning her eyes, her face, her skin, her heart. She could hardly breath anymore. She sank more and more in a dazed sleep from which she thought she would never again awaken.

But she awoke after what seemed ages. She was
lying beside her beloved brother, her head leaning
on his strong shoulder and her happiness was so
great in seeing him again that she could hardly
move.

But she noticed at once that even her brother could not move or greet her cheerfully. They were both captured in a sea-net of green weeds, somewhere at the farthest end of the sea.

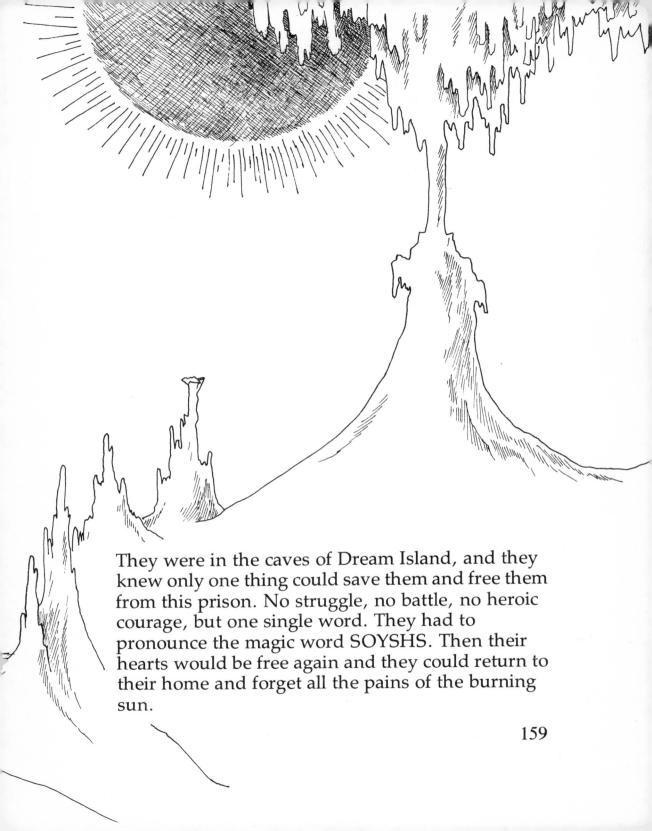

They were in the caves of Dream Island, and they knew only one thing could save them and free them from this prison. No struggle, no battle, no heroic courage, but one single word. They had to pronounce the magic word SOYSHS. Then their hearts would be free again and they could return to their home and forget all the pains of the burning sun.

159

Nobody will ever know if they spoke the magic word and the songs of the three dream-ladies can only reach the mermaids at the bottom of the sea.